Contents

My Pink Stilettos - Spring Edition

"

When people won't give you an opportunity, Create one!

Larita Rice-Barnes
#IWokeUpToPurpose

LIVING OUT LOUD

You can fulfill your wildest dreams. That's what I'm doing! I've decided to live out loud every day, every second, every minute. You know the old saying you get one life so you might as well live it to the fullest. In a healthy and responsible way that is. My Pink Stilettos was a vision that became a dream come true. A vision to bring women together from all across the world. We all have gifts, skills, talents and abilities. There is a tribe that has been assigned to us all. Your tribe knows your vibe and your vibe attracts your tribe. I want to speak into your life. There's absolutely NOTHING that you can not do. You have divinely been given everything that you need to succeed. It lives on the inside of you. It is called dunamis power. It's supernatural. It enables you to run through troops and leap over walls. It aligns you with greatness and it attracts the people, places and things that will help you get to the next level. Living out loud will cause you to lose some friends. But, guess what the ones that you gain will be the ones that you need. Living out loud will require you to walk away from fear. Fear is a thief and enemy to our destinies. Fear Ain't our friend. It's like Aldi the stock up store. It has all of our blessings stored up. Fear sits in our board rooms and make decisions for us. Fear is that door that we allow to keep us from crossing over to the other side. I want to encourage you today to step out and live loud. No fear. No Excuses Just set your mind and do it. The world is waiting on you to show up and show out.

**Editor In Chief
Dr. Larita Rice-Barnes**

When Women Rise

The
Naugles
Family

When
Women Rise

Lisa Nicole Cloud

When Women Rise At first glance you are struck by her exotic beauty. Her mocha colored skin, and long, black, silky hair, makes her appear dressed to rival even the couture fashion. However, one should not be fooled. She is not just another pretty face, nor is she an ordinary beauty. She is a force with a mission. She does not just walk into a room. She makes an entrance. She commands the attention of an audience. As she introduces herself with **bold confidence, you realize** that this woman came to do business.

"Hello, my name is Lisa Nicole," she says, and proceeds her presentation with grit. You lean in to listen closely as her words are not mere emotion. Instead, they are words that come from a place of having goals, direction, commitment, perseverance, passion, and action. "Live your dreams… it is possible." That is Lisa Nicole Cloud.

You may recognize her from

the reality show Married to Medicine. However, before television, Lisa Nicole established herself a woman's woman when she founded WEN (Women's Empowerment Network). WEN is a conference with an impressive platform of successful women teaching, encouraging, and motivating women to live out their purpose. She brings to her panel women at the top of their profession. She only wants the best for those she inspires. She personifies authenticity through her transparent speeches of humble beginnings, setbacks, and never conceding or compromising her dreams. She is proof that with hard work, a bull's eye focus, personal development, and great mentorship, anyone is capable of living the life of their dreams.

I can personally attest to that. I met the petite powerhouse at a conference in Atlanta, GA. I shared with her that I wanted to level up my life both personally and professionally. She listened patiently and invited me to join her on an empowerment call. There was no middleman, and no assistant to make an appointment with. There was simply Lisa offering herself and her time. I was honored and pleasantly surprised that such an accomplished woman would take the time to personally share her wisdom.

Highly educated at Johns-Hopkins University and pre-med at Emory University, Lisa could have chosen a different path. Instead, she incorporated her education into building a successful multilevel marketing business with 5linx. She teaches women the importance of multiple streams of income, wealth trends, and taking control of your own wealth. To ensure the success of those that she mentors, Lisa makes herself easily accessible.

Once she becomes your mentor, Lisa becomes your greatest supporter, coaching by phone, zoom and even flying out of state to assist her mentee.

She guides with perseverance, and never letting go of your hand until you are ready to rise. Your success is her success. She cares about the "whole" woman, including her outer appearance. This led me to discuss her designer clothing line BOSS. BOSS, created with the confident, sophisticated, yet edgy woman in mind, has taken the fashion world by storm. Gracing the runways of New York and Paris, it's receiving rave reviews.

BOSS is not your typical off-the-rack designer line. It is not made through mass production. Boss is handmade on site at the posh showroom. Each piece is unique with intricate detail. It's created by the watchful eyes of the best seamstress in the business. The fabric is of the best quality. It's made from silk, satin, rayon, organza, and many other types of fabric. Her designs range from casual to chic, from simple elegance to extravagant, from day wear to work attire, from showroom pieces to custom couture. Her line does not spare quality in design embellishment of sequins, rhinestones, or pearls. They are carefully sewn into place so that they do not disrupt the fabric but remain firmly in place.

Lisa's BOSS line has graced many national and international runways, but her brightest shine sparkles on runways in Atlanta, Georgia where she promotes local fashion shows with sold out seating to rival that of fashion week in Paris. From the lighting, the music, the décor, the models, even down to the hair and makeup of the models, her shows are professional and top notch. Runways are not her only platform. She does pop-up shops, having traveled as far as Memphis, TN to showcase her collection. When she is not doing runway shows, you can find her at one of her VIP sip and shop gatherings. That brings me to her posh showroom. Decorated with crystal chandeliers, and elegant furnishings, the showroom walls are lined with beautiful clothes scaling from one end of the showroom to the other. There is nothing ordinary about it. The ambiance is more of a high-end boutique than a showroom. Lisa has dressed women from all walks of life including politicians, pastors, even celebrities. Her designs speak to her belief that "When you look good, you feel good." Her love for fashion is clearly shown as each piece is quality made and created from the vision of Lisa Nicole. One would think that such a huge success would be selfishly hoarded. But that's not Lisa. She opened BOSS to other women to serve as brand ambassadors, which allows an additional stream of income. The women are trained with proven strategies, and selling techniques, and are given a generous discount to build their inventory.

With such an impressive education pedigree, a hit reality show, and a self-made millionaire, Lisa Nicole could easily claim the title of "a diva." On the contrary, she is nicknamed "Miss Millionaire Maker," as she does not keep the secret of her success to herself. She has helped many become documented millionaires by teaching them to adopt her methodology. Women come from all over the United States to hear her knowledge of growing wealth trends.

It is obvious that she loves what she does as she displays such passion in speaking, but she also has a personal legacy near and dear to her heart. She teaches and inspires her 13 year old daughter, Amira. She is the spitting image of her mother, smart, bright, and ambitious. She attends some of her mother's conferences and refers to herself as a BOSS woman in the making. Amira has caught the vision of her mother and is sure to follow in her footsteps and continue Lisa's legacy for generations to come.

Her ingenuity of creating "Multiple Streams of Income" has become a staple in empowering women. Having businesses such as 5linx, BOSS clothing line, and recently adding Clinics and Laboratories for COVID 19 testing, has created a solid, consistent flow of finances. In these uncertain times, creating multiple streams of income is a necessary MUST and Lisa Nicole Cloud is definitely the expert to show you how.

BOSS by Lisa Nicole is sure to become an international household name in the fashion industry. With designs to rival that of top designers, she is sure to grow exponentially in the very near future. The lady had a vision, a dream that she made happen. Her success is admirable. She is definitely one to watch as a rising fashion designer. The petite power-house is making her mark and carving a prestigious place for herself in fashion. Lisa Nicole-Cloud is a star, and true to its namesake, a boss. BOSS by Lisa Nicole, that is.

Women Blazing Trails

Asian Women Bossing Up

Sheena Yap Chan

For the longest time, Asian women have been seen by society as quiet, submissive and obedient. Sometimes they are viewed as individuals who are treated as sex objects. Because of this myth, many of the women of my race do not end up in leadership roles, are not treated humanely and become an easy target for hate crimes.

Our upbringing is also part of the problem. Asian women have been taught all their lives to never make any noise, stay in the background and do as you're told. Most of the time, when something bad happens to us, we usually keep it to ourselves. This is because we don't want to cause trouble for our families even when it isn't our fault.

Considering what has been happening to our Asian community with the rise of Asian-targeted hate crimes, especially against women who are 2.3 times more likely to be a victim of a hate crime, it is necessary now more than ever to speak up. We need to create resources that showcase a strong representation of Asian women.

This is why we have to change the way society sees Asian women and build them up. For the past 5 years, I have been creating a stronger representation of Asian women through my podcast called, "The Tao of Self-Confidence." Through this podcast, I interview Asian women about their journey to self-confidence. I have interviewed over 700 Asian women from around the world about this topic.

Since a podcast was not enough to create the representation needed, we came out with our own book titled "Asian Women Who Boss Up." In this publication, we highlight 18 stories of Asian women explaining how they are able to forge their path, overcome obstacles and thrive. This book is so important because you never see books that highlight 16 amazing Asian women on the front cover. Seeing this book for the first time was like watching Crazy Rich Asians on the big screen for the first time. I was just super happy and super proud that we had our community responsibly represented.

It's also time to change the narrative of Asian women, by saying we are strong, powerful and brave. Because we truly are. As an Asian woman, you are so capable beyond measure to create the life that you want but it's how you see yourself that stops you from your greatness. I hope by reading this, you are able to just take one step forward towards your destiny. Make 2021 the year of the Boss Up!

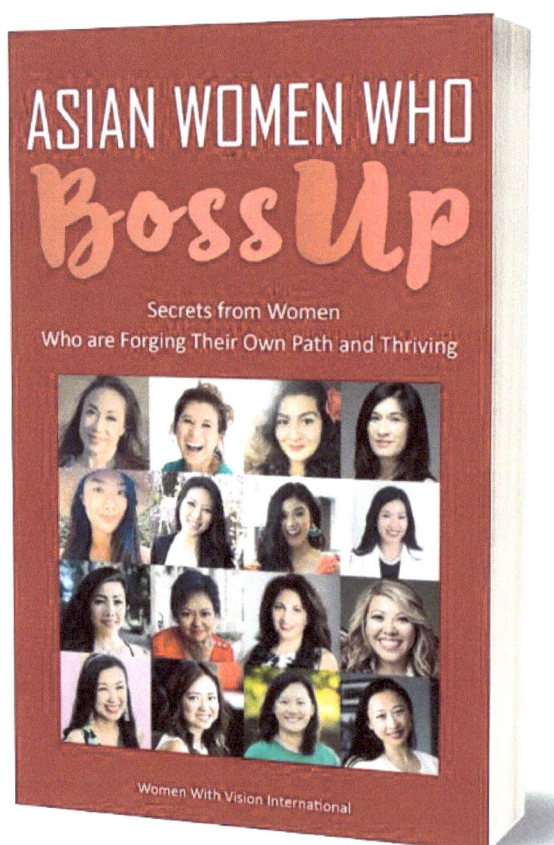

ASIAN WOMEN WHO Boss Up

Secrets from Women Who are Forging Their Own Path and Thriving

Women With Vision International

Thriving In The Fight

Denise Padin Collazo

A Survival Manual for Latinas on the Front Lines of Change

Social justice work is more crucial than ever, but it can be physically and emotionally draining. Longtime activist Denise Collazo offers three keys to help Latinas keep their focus, morale, and energy high.

Doing the work of social change is hard. Waking up every day to take on the biggest challenges of our time can be overwhelming. Sometimes progress is hard to see. She understands that Latina and all women of color activists do their best work when they are thriving, not simply surviving.

Drawing on her own experiences of triumph and failure, and those of other Latina activists, Collazo lays out three keys to thriving in the movement for social change. Activists must lead into their vision, live to become the fullest version of themselves, and love past negatives that hold them back.

Denise Padín Collazo is the senior advisor for external affairs and director of institutional advancement at Faith in Action, the nation's largest faith-based, progressive organizing network. While there, she has advanced the cause of social justice over the past twenty-five years. She is also an official member of the Forbes Nonprofit Council, an invitation-only organization for executives in successful nonprofit organizations.

Link to Denise's Website: DeniseCollazo.com

Prosperando en la lucha: Un manual de supervivencia para las Latinas a la vanguardia del cambio
Hoy día el trabajo por la justicia social es más crucial que nunca. Si bien a menudo es alegre y estimulante, también puede ser agotador física y emocionalmente. Denise Padín Collazo comparte sus propias experiencias de triunfo y fracaso para animar a las Latinas y a todas las mujeres de color a abrazar las tres claves para prosperar en la lucha: liderar desde tu visión, vivir en la versión más completa de ti misma y amar los negativos del pasado que te retienen. Este es un libro honesto, práctico e inspirador que te ayudará a brillar, no a agotarte.

Denise Padín Collazo es una líder de la justicia social, mentora para otras mujeres de color e innovadora en la integración del trabajo y la familia. Se desempeña como asesora principal de asuntos externos en Faith in Action, una red progresista internacional compuesta por 3,000 congregaciones y 2 millones de miembros.

Enlace a su página de web:
DeniseCollazo.com

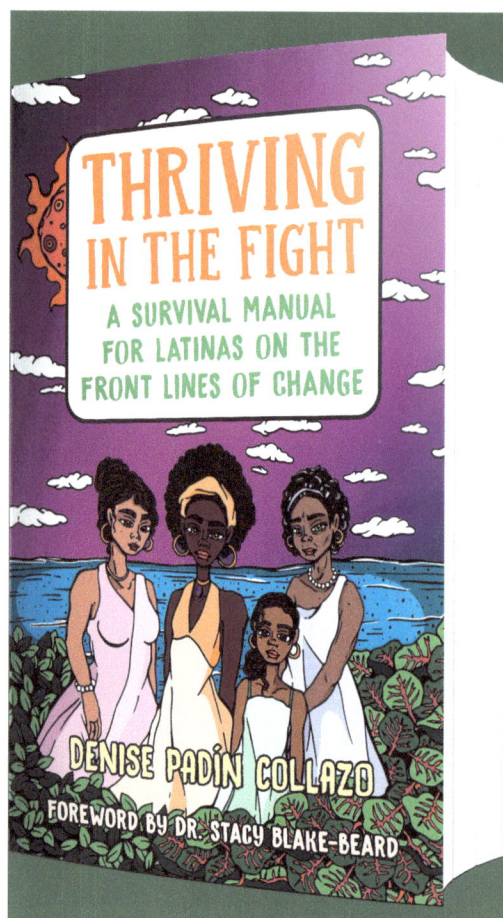

Health
&
Wellness

The Aftermath Of Surviving Covid 19

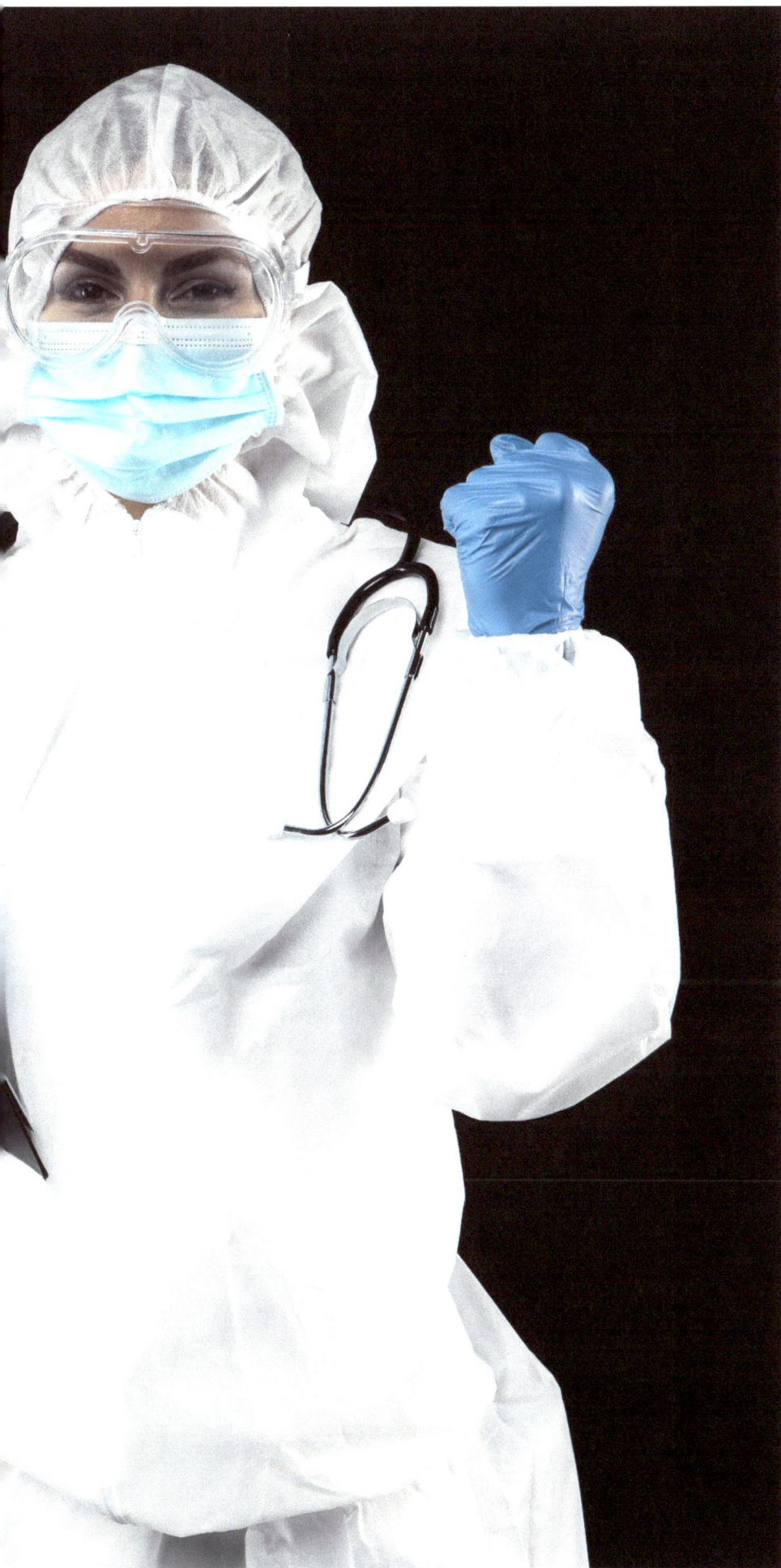

It spewed from my mouth with the force of water from a fire hose. I experienced both the vomiting, and the projectile vomiting, as the symptoms of COVID-19.

I woke up on a Saturday morning feeling fine. However, when I took a sip of my coffee, it had no taste or smell. It dawned on me that I had not smelled the coffee brewing. I sniffed a few more items and there was no smell. I woke my husband and told him that we needed to have a COVID test right away.

We sat in the Urgent Care waiting for the nurse to come out and administer the test. She told us it would be about 15 minutes before she would have the results. We waited patiently in complete silence. We didn't say one word to each other. A nurse came out of the side door gowned, gloved, and masked. She walked over to our car and handed us a document and said, "You are both positive for COVID 19." She asked us how we could have been exposed, and gave us strict instructions to quarantine ourselves for 10-14 days. I did not panic because I felt fine. I thought that I would be one of the lucky ones; other than no taste or smell, I would remain asymptomatic. No such luck. By 8 p.m., I felt weak and nauseous. A few minutes later, I began to throw up. At first, it was a little, then, the flood gates opened. Projectile vomit spewed from my mouth like water from a fire hose. I sat on the couch with a lined wastebasket, when I could not make it to the bathroom. I sipped on water and Gatorade to stay hydrated, but nothing would stay down. I was throwing up so profusely that my son gave me a pillow for my knees as I knelt over the toilet. This went on until the next morning. I could not take it anymore. I went to the Emergency Room where I was placed in an isolation room. An I.V. was started with fluids and medicine for nausea and vomiting. My body was throbbing with pain and I was given pain meds by I.V. as well. I threw up a few more times before the vomiting stopped.

By the time I stopped vomiting, I had a dry cough. The doctor brushed it off as a non-malignant COVID symptom and gave me a prescription for cough medicine with codeine, and something for nausea. I coughed the entire ride home. My body hurt all over, as if someone had thrown my body against a wall. Fast forward. After two emergency visits X-rays detected left upper and lower lobe pneumonia, biomarkers indicating blood clots in my lungs, oxygen saturation of 80% (normal 96-100%), becoming extremely short of breath and unable to speak without coughing.

The doctors were coming in my room every day to tell me, "We just don't know what your outcome will be." I spent ten days in the hospital before I was discharged. They sent me home with oxygen and instructions to lie on my stomach and to use my deep breathing exerciser every hour. I was still very short of breath and my chest felt like an elephant was sitting on it, but I was determined to get better as quickly as possible. I followed the doctor's instructions, took immune boosting and anti-inflammatory vitamins, and did my breathing exercises. After three weeks, it was time for my post COVID hospitalization follow up. I was excited but still on oxygen as. However, I felt 100% better. My appointment required blood work to be done, but I was not the least concerned. After three days, I received a call from the nurse telling me that the doctor wanted me to come in the next day because there were several abnormalities with my blood work. The next day I sat in a room with the Doctor.

She had a very concerned look on her face. She said, "Sweetheart, you are sick. Here are your laboratory results." She read all of the levels of a complete blood count.

I listened in disbelief as she read the results that sounded more like the results of an 80 year old than that of a 53 year old. My laboratory results showed that I was "thrombotic," which means I was high risk for developing blood clots in my legs, and lungs. My cholesterol was 400(normal is less than 200), my lipid ratio was extremely high, indicating that I could have a heart attack at any time, and my A1C was almost 8 indicating that I had diabetes. To add insult to injury the doctor told me that I would experience fatigue, headaches, brain-fog, and shortness of breath for the next six to eight months. She said that COVID-19 damaged my lung with scar tissue, which would make it easy for me to over-exert myself just doing simple tasks.

"What is all this, and where did it come from?" I asked. I was healthy prior to COVID. What the hell is going on? She said that I had POST COVID SYNDROME. I was a LONG HAULER. She explained that those who contracted COVID and required hospitalization were experiencing ongoing symptoms months after being COVID free. Sure, they had anti-bodies, but the virus wreaks havoc on the entire body. It effects not just the lungs but the heart, the circulatory system, the kidneys, the metabolic system, and the brain. I was astonished that I had never heard of such. I felt angry, and disappointed. Before COVID, I was about to embark on a new chapter in my life, in a new location, and a new job. Now all of that would have to wait. The doctor explained to me that very few people knew about POST COVID SYNDROME because the primary focus of treatment was to keep people alive. With COVID being a new virus, there just was not enough scientific knowledge about it. During a pandemic, the after-affects are not top priority. I felt slighted that I was ignorant about the lethal symptoms that could possibly take my life. I survived COVID, but I have a long road of recovery ahead. I researched as much as I could about COVID-19 and POST COVID SYNDROME. My findings were shocking. The COVID virus is a beast. From the very entrance into the body, its intent is to take you out. It's not a cut and dry, one and done virus that infiltrates one organ. It strategically attacks several vital system increasing the chance of morbidity. The body has been taken hostage with no intentions of ever letting it go. Killing is what it is there for. The most obvious treated symptom, pneumonia, is a distraction from all the other deadly damage that it is doing to the body. It is methodical. Surviving COVID-19 is just the beginning, several patients report having symptoms for months afterward. They experience symptoms such as fatigue, chest pain, joint pain, shortness of breath, blood clots, post COVID diabetes, irregular heartbeat and kidney malfunctions. These patients are called "long haulers."

There is no definitive duration of how long symptoms will last. It is different for everyone. There is no rhyme or reason for why one patient suffers a fatal heart attack, and another only fatigue. I found nothing in my research that would shed light on distinguishing factors of symptom susceptibility. Until there is more research about POST COVID SYNDROME, the best that can be done is to make the public aware that it exists. I predict that it will not be any time soon as the COVID 19 numbers continue to rise, and the death toll climbs. It does not leave much room to give attention to secondary illness.
Written by-

Paula Thornton-Campbell

Beauty
&
Brains

Nicole Beauty and Wellness Expert

The Art of Make-Up

In my 10 years as a makeup artist, I have had the privilege to service women with just about every skin tone, type, and a vast number of skin concerns. A lot of people don't know that your face can tell a lot about what is going on inside the body. Putting on a little makeup not only enhances your mood, confidence, and overall appearance, it can actually save your life! Okay, maybe that's a little dramatic, but you'll see what I mean if you keep reading.

Applying makeup makes you pay special attention to your skin. If you apply foundation, you may notice if your skin is hyper pigmented, and if there are dark spots that are hard to cover. These dark spots can indicate that you need to add sunscreen to your skin care regimen, add a night treatment with retinol to speed up the skins cell turnover (healing process), or simply stop popping your pimples.

Definitely try the above suggested treatments, but, while your skin is healing itself to cover the dark spots, you can utilize a technique called 'color correcting.' What color correcting does is cancel out the pigment that is making a spot appear a different shade than your overall skin complexion. For very fair complexions with extreme redness, an olive under toned veil of a color correcting product will cancel out the redness. In the case of most black women, a concealer with a warm (red or orange) under tone, will brighten the dark spots to look identical to the healthier areas of your skin.

Now, on a more serious note, spending a little time to put on makeup in the morning will make you see if your color is drastically changing without excessive sun exposure. This could be an indicator of hormonal changes, liver issues, thyroid issues, and more. You want to visit a doctor in this case.

Breakouts are also more noticeable when you're giving your face more attention. They can be indicators that adjustments are needed. For some, dairy, chocolate, and soda can cause breakouts anywhere on the face. If your breakouts are concentrated below the nose, you should examine your stress levels. This area is where stress breakouts take place. Deep breathing, yoga, walking, stretching, and quiet time can help manage stress.

We get so busy managing our lives like Wife-ing, Slaying, Mom-ing, and Bossing. Some of us have gotten comfortable using dove soap on our faces and running out the house to save the world. While I celebrate how dedicated you are to your loved ones, I invite you to take a few minutes for yourself in the morning. You see, putting on a little makeup in the morning is more than just for glam. While you will inevitably feel more confident and beautiful, taking the time to really SEE yourself in the mornings is the wellness check that could, very well, enhance your overall health and well-being.

NICOLE
BEAUTY & WELLNESS EXPERT

Meet CJH!

Beauty & Brains

Canesha (CJH Brand) Henry

If you're natural and in this case meaning no relaxers, you've probably become a researcher, scientist, stylist and chemist by now! We are in the age of influencers, and vloggers and there's content being created everywhere to tell you everything you should be doing with your hair. You've probably read that you should only use sulfate-free shampoo. Let me just tell you why this is a BIG no in my salon. Sulfate is a cleansing agent that is used to deeply clarify the scalp and de-clog cuticles. Sure, after shampooing your hair it'll feel much dryer, but that's because you've stripped your hair of buildup and debris. To add natural oils and vitamins in your hair you should always follow up with a conditioner. Your shampoo and conditioning process is way more important than any other product you can buy. This is oftentimes what everyone is less likely to invest in. This can help prevent excessive shedding, breakage and dryness. Sulfate-free shampoo should not be your main shampoo.

BONUS TIP: Shampoo with warm water and rinse your conditioner with cool water*

About the Founder

It's unbelievable that this Jackson State, Dean's List, Criminal Justice major is now working full time as a Brand and Image Consultant under her own business, CJH Brand. Although Canesha had a complete career change she considers herself a permanent student and uses her academic foundation in psychology and sociology while staying up to date with the latest marketing strategies through continuing education and personal development. In just 4 short years she has worked on play sets, movie sets, she's worked with your favorite artists, and TV and radio personalities. CJ has been featured on platforms like the Grio, ReV Air, St Louis Public radio and more. She helps to cultivate and monetize skills her clients have by way of coaching and counseling. She is known for her creative ideas, faith and wisdom. CJ passionately works to improve brands professionally and personally to attract the money you want to make. If you're planning to launch a business or you're in limbo with the one you have now contact me. Let's get started and let's get solid!

www.cjhbrand.com
FB @cjhbrand
IG @cjhbrand

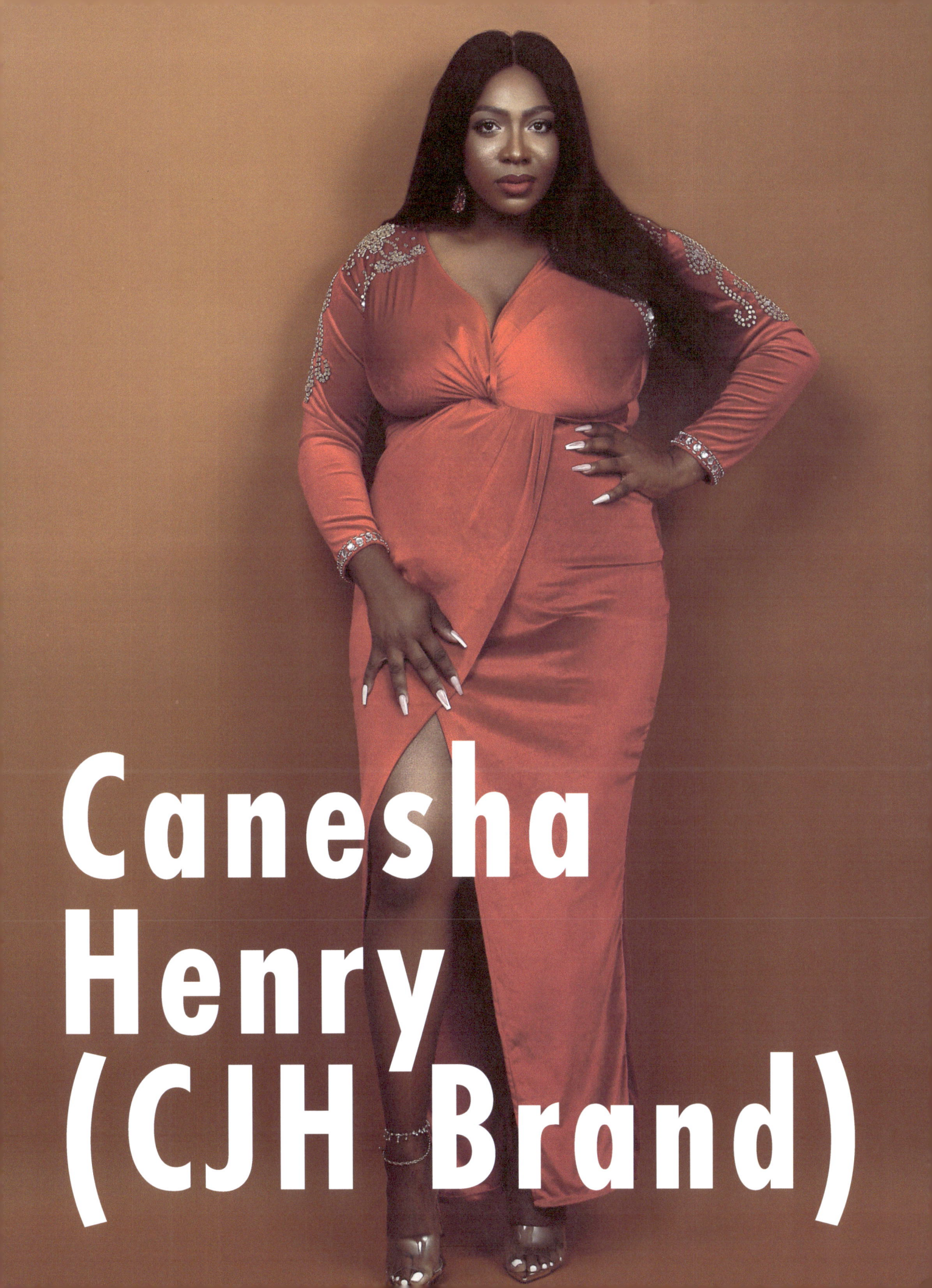

Canesha
Henry
(CJH Brand)

Authors Spotlight

My name is **Rebecca McClain** and I am CEO of Pure Perfection LLC. I'm a wife, and mother of five! I have three girly girls and two boys. Fashion is my passion. I love helping others. Clothing is only a portion of what my company provides. We promote boldness, beauty, elegance, and confidence too!

Contact us by IG @ **pure_perfection6**

Facebook @ **Pure Perfection**

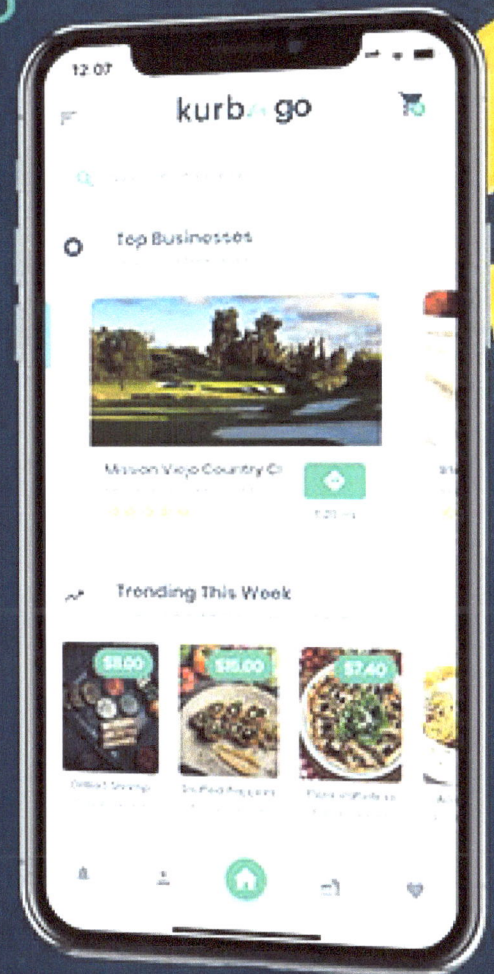

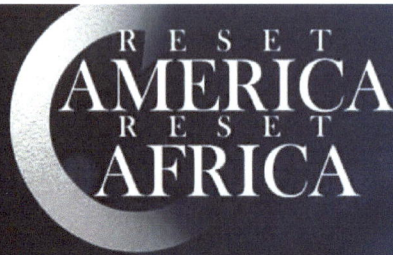

GLOBAL IMPACT LEADERSHIP ALLIANCE

OUR VISION

Our vision is to support and connect developing countries through economic development, advocacy through legislation, fund development, and spiritual growth; with a focus on enhancement through our innovative ideas we will increase economic development through the import and export of goods and services.

KEY AREAS

GILA has strategically identified key leaders from across the globe who are skilled in their crafts and have a passion to lead, train and develop world-class leaders. Our focus is to dominate the 7 areas of influence, which are:

BUSINESS | ARTS & ENTERTAINMENT | MEDIA | GOVERNMENT | FAMILY | EDUCATION | RELIGION

www.globalimpactnow.org
media@globalimpactnow.org